Advance Praise for

In *Beneath a Strawberry Night Sky*, Robin Michel asks: "Will poetry redeem anyone?" The poems offer a powerful response. These are personal, narrative poems that seek redemption in their honest examinations of a life. They speak not only to poetry but to domesticity, motherhood, and marriage—squarely facing the limits and ends of love. In descriptive, moving poems, Michel reflects on the 'tightrope' between being 'trapped' and 'free,' between what we 'possess' and 'desire.'
—Shara McCallum, *No Ruined Stone* and *Madwoman*

Robin Michel's debut collection of poetry is a daunting, imagistic perusal of the reasons we leave the womb of lost desire. Neither a reproach nor a celebration, *Beneath a Strawberry Night Sky*, is a look at the underside of the known world, where everyone is at fault, there are no clear solutions, and the painful beauty of the search is all that is left.
—Indigo Moor, *Everybody's Jonesin' for Something*, *In the Room of Thirsts & Hungers*, *Through the Stonecutter's Window*, and *Tap-Root*

I opened Robin Michel's *Beneath a Strawberry Night Sky* planning to read a handful of the poems but I couldn't stop until I read them all. Her subjects are illuminated moments of the joys, sorrows, and mysteries of family life and of the natural world. These words, spare and beautiful, call forth the memories of the reader in a breathtaking way. Her poems are wise and powerful.
—Lynne Kaufman, Playwright and Novelist

Robin Michel's moving and authentic poetry resonates with me deeply. The poems deftly capture the experience of divorce and its impacts on the family in a compassionate, honest, and reflective manner. I would recommend *Beneath a Strawberry Night Sky* to all family law practitioners, especially those just starting out.
—Christopher J. Donnelly, Family Law Attorney (retired) and SFUSD Law Academy Mentor

Robin Michel's courageous poems in *Beneath a Strawberry Night Sky* take us on a journey of inner and outer worlds. A woman not living fully in a marriage, questioning each room, worrying about each child. A toddler counting stars, and a woman counting the days. A journey many of us have made or will make, this book acknowledges our collective hurt, and hope, as we tightrope our way to a new life…poems filled with honest emotion and the details of daily life expressed in stunning images: a spider lurking beneath a strawberry leaf, children building 'traps,' and a marriage bed too small or too big. I couldn't put down this book filled with self-knowledge and such large questions. These poems recognize the shape-shifting nature of love and the way poetry saves us.
—Angie Minkin, *A Balm for the Living*

It is a marvel to witness the exploration of pain and joy as a marriage ends in Robin Michel's *Beneath a Strawberry Night Sky*. Many readers will find a place for themselves in her skillful poetry…I find my own memories brightly illuminated and in that bright light, reach a greater understanding. When a mother imagines renouncing "fluorescent lights and masked doctors" to fiercely give bloody birth in the wild woods, I am there with her. While searching for a daughter alone on an overpass at 2 AM, it is love that pulls the mother—and the reader—out of despair. Flowing through these years are intriguing images of love and friendship… and always, a return to the grounding process of poetry."
—Heather Saunders Estes, *All In Measure: A Book of Hours 2020-2022, Cloudbreak,* and *Inner Sunset*

Beneath a Strawberry Night Sky

Robin Michel

Fremont, California

Copyright 2023 by Robin Michel
All rights reserved

Printed in the United States of America

Cover: *Erdbeeren (Strawberries),* 1820, a painting by Johann Adam Schlesinger. Public Domain.
Author Photo: Mimi Carroll
Illustration, page 50: *Fragaria, Longworth,* 1912, by Amanda Almira Newton, U.S. Department of Agriculture Pomological Watercolor Collection. Rare and Special Collections, National Agricultural Library, Beltsville, MD 20705

The text of this book is composed in Adobe Garamond Pro.
Library of Congress Control Number: 2023945642
ISBN: 978-1-7337289-3-5

Acknowledgements

Thank you to the following publications and their editors where these poems, or earlier versions of these poems, first appeared:

Journal of Family Life: "A Poem for My Son While He Sleeps"
Kumquat Meringue: "Letter to the Editor"
The MacGuffin: "Riding South on Interstate 70"
Northampton Poetry Review: "Some Days"
Poetry Forum: "Deferred Desire"
Rappahannock Review: "At the Psychiatrist's Office"
Remembering: "In Our Marriage Bed"
Sisyphus: "Reading Your Morning Horoscope," "Writing Seduction Letters"
South 85 Journal: "Escalon, Past the Orchards"
Still Points Art Quarterly: "Second Chance Dance" published as "Dance Lesson"
Switchgrass Volume 5: "Factors and Exponents"
Three by Three: "Remembering Birch Lake"
Toho Journal: "Just Like That"
The Union Democrat: "Counting Stars"

*for Mary, Jesse, and Samantha—
and for their father*

Contents

Prologue / xi
The Invasive Nature of Ivy / 1
Bleeding Strawberries / 2
Summer at Birch Lake / 3
Counting Stars / 4
The Tooth / 5
The Housewife Surveys Her Surroundings / 6
Deferred Desire / 7
A Poem for My Son While He Sleeps / 8
Traps / 9
Without a Net / 10
Fishing Alameda Creek With Our Nine-Year-Old Son / 11
Escalon, Past the Orchards / 12
In Our Marriage Bed / 13
Being the Woman Who Smiles / 14
Exit Signs / 15
Factors and Exponents / 16
Some Days / 18
Second Chance Dance / 19
My Husband, His Wife / 20
While Driving Back Home From the Orthodontist / 21
Letter to the Editor / 22
Writing Seduction Letters / 23
Reading Your Morning Horoscope / 24
Driving the Utah Desert, Children in the Backseat / 25

At a Rest Stop Between Butte and Missoula / 26
Coos Bay, Oregon / 27
Why She Bought the Poet's Book / 28
But for the Lovers, Their Arms / 29
Blackberries / 30
What a Poem Cannot Do / 31
White Clouds / 32
Avalanche / 34
Riding South on Interstate 70 / 35
Damaged Proof / 36
Young Girl Lost on the Overpass / 37
An Empty Table and Abandoned Chairs / 38
The Uncoupling / 39
Strawberries / 40
I Thought It Was Over Long Before It Was Done / 41
Bone, Exposed / 42
Just Like That / 44
Everyone Wants What They Want / 45
At the Psychiatrist's Office / 46
Thanksgiving Table / 48
Remembering Birch Lake / 49
Botanical Illustration: Frageria, Longworth / 50
Epilogue / 51
A Brief Note of Thanks from the Poet / 53

Prologue

First Night
I wake from the dream, weeping.
You hold me close. "What is it?"
"I couldn't marry you." We talk.
No, I talk. You listen. Until exhausted,
we both fall into a troubled sleep,
broken once again when the newspaper
skids across our front porch.

Second Night
Your silence startles me awake.
I listen for your ragged breathing.
Hearing nothing, I lean into your
chest, comforted by its rise and fall.
The blackout shade shuts out the moon's
soft light. If I slept alone, the curtain
would never be drawn.

Third Night
I dream of my ex-husband.
We are still married. Still miserable.
Waking, I kiss your sleeping cheek.
Bereft. Consoled. Confused.

The Invasive Nature of Ivy

Like trying to find a secret key
in a children's puzzle book, I looked hard to see
patches of scarlet fiberglass between the ivy's dark leaves.

The canoe was free with a camper purchase,
and you unceremoniously tipped it upside down
in a far corner of our back yard under the loquat tree.
Upside down to prevent the kids from climbing aboard
and sailing on pretend seas to battle pirates or visit distant lands.

How many times did I suggest we take the children and our
canoe—or was it yours?—on the lake before I stopped asking?

It never occurred to me to go it alone. In those days,
I didn't drive freeways, or even know how to pump my own gas.
A wasted asset.

Ivy is invasive. Aggressive and smothering.
I've learned its old names: *Bindwood* and *Lovestone.*

The ivy grew as quick as resentments, wrapping its tendrils
around the boat, climbing up the tree's trunk, its heart-leaves
mingling with phallic-shaped leaves and golden globes of fruit.

Twenty-two years now since our divorce.
I still remember the first time we made love.

Now I remember how we sat at a table with our attorneys
dividing up our shared property—our shared life—and I asked
you for the canoe. You refused.

Is it still tipped upside down beneath the loquat tree, strangled in ivy?

Bleeding Strawberries

Cupid draws from his quiver
a slender, silver arrow.
His aim is straight.
Pierces to the quick.
My heart freely bleeds
red juices of strawberries
picked on a joyous
summer's afternoon.
Beneath a trembling leaf,
beware the spider.

Summer at Birch Lake

Bright spots of white light
float on moss-brown pond
and a band of rag-tag children
gather at the water's edge
to build a civilization
all their own
mud squishes
between their toes
sand tattoos decorate
their arms and backs
and many, as if peeling off
layers of old skin, shed their clothes

frogs no bigger than their thumbs   leap
from their grasp to temporary safety
        —a rock, a twig, a leaf—

mud-streaked bodies & sun-streaked hair
sweet faces solemn beneath the stipple of mud
all working together
    side by side
        age height gender
            no determiner of power
                as if Equals in Paradise.

Counting Stars

"One...two...free...five...ten..."

    Beneath a Strawberry night sky
    she and I count stars.
        Distant bluegrass and new grass
            merge into a carousel's calliope
of circus tunes: fiddles, guitars, banjos, and the riotous
        hoots and hollers swell into a chorus of angels,
            a heavenly drunken choir.

"ten...free...five...one...two...free...ten..."

    She points, each star a startling light
        pricking the inky dark.
No star too small to count.
No job too big, now that she is two fingers old.
Her feet poke out beneath her blanket.
Still, she fits in my arms. Still.
    Her weight nestles beneath my chest.
        Cold air tickles our noses.

"Too many," she sighs. Rubs her eyes.

I remind her, "Not if we count only ten at a time."

    She begins again, "One...two...ten...free...two..."

    free...
        in a way we seldom are at home
            where we forget to count stars.

The Tooth

You open wide your mouth and expose the empty space where moments before one small white tooth dangled from a tiny bleeding thread. I watch you wash it more thoroughly than you have ever brushed it when still attached, turning it over in your hands, marveling at its shape. Smaller than your littlest fingernail, one side worn down, the hollow emptied of its nerve, dried blood embedded in its crevices. "It's so sharp," you whisper, let me touch it. It reminds me of a tiny shell you once found washed upon a beach, pocketed, treasured. Earlier I offered to pull the loose tooth for you, but you refused. Later, thinking of finding all that silver under your pillow in exchange for one small tooth, you worried it free with a violent yank of your own small hand. "No," you say, "I'm keeping it." I watch you roll this tiny piece of calcified tissue between thumb and forefinger, staring at it as if trying to understand the all too brief moment of possession. The reluctance of letting go.

The Housewife Surveys Her Surroundings

Living inside these walls
one hallway connecting the separate
compartments of my life: kitchen bedroom bath

I find I am rootless here
and I am not sheltered   but encased   held tight
by these walls   this ceiling   this floor

I could be windowless
for I seldom remember the openings
in the walls which I could throw open
and crawl outside to find wide blue
cool spaces and an unsealed sky above

I have mostly forgotten the earthy cool
iron smell of dirt and the sun's
itching warmth upon bare shoulders to remind
me I have blood that flows like a river through my body
and skin that responds to stimuli
and a voice to be used out loud

Inside these walls, I forget
that I am more than a function
within this home.

Inside these walls,
I forget that I am more.

Deferred Desire

When did logistics get in the way of lovemaking,
or the proper amount of sleep so important?
When did work, tending to children,
reading newspapers, watching TV,
pursuing hobbies, and meeting commitments
outside our intertwining lives take such precedence,
leaving us exhausted, pent-up, and emptied?
You say you are going to bed—look at me
a full second longer than usual.
Saying goodnight, I barely glance at you.
I stay motionless on the couch,
inwardly reeling from a child's tantrum
that escalated into child-parent / parent-parent
confrontations. Your footsteps fade down the hallway.
I remember some sleepy promise we made to one another
the night before in our bed, too tired to stoke our dim fire.
Understanding the pause before you went to bed,
I feel guilt, but it is not enough.
Does desire, too often postponed, dry up,
leaving us, though love exists, as brother and sister?
My body sags upon the bed,
craving the passion we once knew,
with no concern but one another and our pleasure.
And I wonder, is there sex after children?
And does desire too often postponed,
dry up, leaving us, though love exists,
as brother and sister?

A Poem for My Son While He Sleeps

You will grow apart from me
when you become a man and speak a language
I do not understand.

Will you laugh at the games we shared
when you were just a little boy?
Will you remember?

Picking up a stick you point. I fall to the ground.
You run and cover my face in kisses. I rise and hug you,
twisting the lone curl hidden beneath new grown hair.

Who will tire of these games first?

Your face sweetly curved, your skin free of marks.
I watch your sleeping breath gently rise and fall
beneath your breast. You are my son. I am your mother.

How quickly will you leave?

Earlier while watching a film about a mother who
abandons home and leaves her child in another woman's arms,
I caught you watching me through half-concealed eyes.

"You cry at everything, and it isn't even sad."

"You would cry, too, if you were older."

Traps

They build traps:
leprechaun traps, lizard traps, mouse traps,
deer traps, squirrel traps, moose traps.
Elaborate, colorful things
out of shoe and cereal boxes,
berry baskets and coffee cans,
rubber bands, glue, rocks, tape.
Two heads, bent low,
his dark, hers fair,
arranging blades of grass for deer,
gold glitter for leprechauns,
bits of cheese, stale bread,
marshmallows, small pieces of gum.
Always, they discuss, plan,
and think of the comfort and needs
of their soon-to-be captives:
a soft bed, fresh water, decorations
drawn boldly upon with scented markers.
Rainbows are especially good for leprechauns.
Who would not fall for such a trap?
Who would not love it, and so love its architects?
I watch them. Think of curtains not stirring
in the hot, still air,
dinner on the table,
a man mowing his lawn,
children building traps.

Without a Net

In this dark house
I find myself thinking
of bright lights and circuses

how I artfully arrange
my face each morning
paint on a smile
or act a clown

how some days
I must tame the lions,
trembling
with fake bravado

how I walk
down this path between
what I possess and what I desire
like a tightrope walker
maintaining
a graceless balance

as part of me
watches
from the stands,
a spectator holding her breath,
and I fall
               without a net.

Fishing Alameda Creek With Our Nine-Year-Old Son

"What a glorious vision I see....a large, fat fish on a china plate, resting in an ocean of lemon juice and butter sauce."
—Arnold Lobel, "The Cat and His Visions" from *Fables*

Just the two of us, a creek ten minutes from our house.
I took a book and he carried his rod and reel,
a cheap plastic tackle box filled with small jars
of lumpy orange cheese and fluorescent marshmallows,
a proud assortment of lures and hooks.
"How does it feel to be a fisherman?" I asked.
He grinned, his eyes flashing the sheen of a blue-bellied skink.
I watched him bait his hook and tried not to flinch
as it pierced the body of his wriggling worm—

I had fished but once in my life,
about the age my son is now. My grandfather
steadied my hands on the rod, helped me reel it in.
I cried when the four-inch rainbow trout
glistened on the boat's deck,
struggled for breath. I pleaded with my grandfather.
"Cut it free!" He refused. "Once hooked," he said,
"it will bleed to death."

Escalon, Past the Orchards

In Escalon past orchards sandwiched between
modest tract homes, a man sits hunched over
beside the railroad tracks as if waiting for a train.

He wears navy slacks, a short-sleeved shirt; and his hair
is neatly cut, military style. Some old man, a stranger
by the tracks, head bent low, face hidden.

He is a familiar to me. How often have I seen this man before?
Where was he born? Where is he going? Who—or what—
is he waiting for?

"Escalon, my grandfather was born here, I think,"
says my husband as we drove past the orchards, the houses,
the railroad tracks, the waiting man.

I look back to the old man, who could be my husband's
Portuguese grandfather born in Escalon, California,
more than eighty years ago, now waiting to die

in a big city hospital while a stranger's blood pumps
through his veins, born in this dusty little rail-track town
but claiming the Azores Islands as his native soil.

The old man, no longer visible through our car's rear window.
Like all of us, marking time.

In Our Marriage Bed

In our marriage bed,
when first we fought,
it seemed as if our mattress grew too small
to hold our growing bodies.
Squirming to avoid one another,
a leg, thigh, arm or shoulder would accidentally touch,
and we would move away, offended.

This same double bed
has now moved with us from apartment
to apartment, house to house.
We often talked about buying a new bed,
debating king or queen, firm mattress, pillow top, or coil,
postponing this purchase for more important things:
a crib, children's bicycles, a reliable car, braces.

These nights, we no longer fight.
Our bed has grown to accommodate
our changing bodies. It could now contain
an entire world between us.
We sleep with no bridge between.

We are not at war.
We are not at peace.
We remain neutral; keep our positions to ourselves.
And having learned to coexist, we are indifferent.

Our people do not visit one another,
exchange customs, or take back souvenirs.

Our bodies never touch.

Being the Woman Who Smiles

Going through the motions,
I remind myself that I am the woman
who smiles at those who pass by,
knowing that no light radiates from within.

I look at a white twig, a blade of yellow grass,
a blushing apple ripe upon the dark brown earth.
I know that these things are inherently beautiful—
feel nothing.

My young, blonde daughter who walks beside me
holding my hand offers comfort.
She is the green, slender stem I hang onto,
afraid it will break beneath so much weight.

Exit Signs

How many miles did I ride in the passenger seat
counting road signs, trees, buildings, overpasses, and exits—
anything to drown out the silence of the man
behind the steering wheel or his angry complaints?

How many times did my own grievance
clamber into the front seat and lodge itself between us,
a third passenger grumbling about the stick shift
bruising her tender leg?

Long are the miles we traveled through this familiar landscape.
With radio blaring, I practiced numbness, played road games,
adopted a false detachment—anything to keep my anger
in check.

Anything to keep me from swinging open the car door.
Jumping out. Anything to keep me from finding my own way.

Factors and Exponents

I sat at the table with our children
doing homework as you walked past
popping the top of your beer can.
Cringing at the sound,
I waited for your anger
to surface like empty, useless foam
as you made your exodus
into the garage.
Our son gripped his pencil
in unskilled fist, scratching out
prime factors and exponents.
Our daughter buried her head
deep in a book on DNA
as we struggled to understand.
I expected the blare of stereo
to signal your cool retreat
as you gathered intense white heat
to once again approach and attack.

Instead, the plaintive notes of a guitar
too long ignored slid beneath the closed
kitchen door, and your voice
floats in, brighter than the tiny sliver
of light it cuts through, filling the room with ghosts.
I remember fragments of dreams—
someone I love has died and now returns.
In these dreams I am cautious.
"I thought you were dead—"
"Oh no! It was all a mistake."
I am radiant in their resurrection.
Your voice, so long absent,

is like this dream. Its honey spreads out
and fills the kitchen.

This is the way I always imagined it—
the warm womb of a bright kitchen,
you filling our house with song,
me writing poetry,
our children holding their pencils
in relaxed hands, reading aloud,
asking questions, expressing ideas.

Some Days

Some days you hear
a bit of music that feels
like rain. Like rain, your heart breaks,
but never mind. The ache is a part of you
and beyond you, too. Like the rain.
Open wide and round your mouth,
let it pour inside you.
You want to swallow it.
You want to be swallowed by it.
And all that really matters is
this ache of beauty
that will not let you go.
>*Tell me, do you really want it to?*
>*Will you ever know?*

Some days you hear
a bit of music that feels like rain,
and the drops scatter
across your thirsting skin
like thousands of teasing promises
whispered from invisible lips
and wings, whether you believe
in such things or not.
And all that really matters
is this eternal ache of beauty that ends,
and comes again and again.

Second Chance Dance

Tonight
      as tears fall
           we don't stop
to pick them up

      or try to explain

          we don't stop dancing

    one-two-three-four
                        one-two-three-four

    small steps we should have learned long ago

    one-two-three-four

My Husband, His Wife

My Husband
He sleeps his breath deep body heavy.
A man's home is his castle.
The night rusts away his armor
and the world moves on around him.

His Wife
What do I want packing my mind
like a suitcase and booking a flight
to who knows where while my body sits
in front of the computer screen growing cobwebs?

While Driving Back Home From the Orthodontist

I mentally tick off our obligatory promises:
    I promise to write a check for car insurance.
    You promise to to change the oil.
    I promise to return your mother's phone call.
    You promise to not be late for our son's baseball game.
We no longer make promises of undying love—

Our oldest daughter interupts my thoughts.

    "My friend Sarah's parents are getting divorced."

The news hangs in the air,
    a bruised and bloated balloon begging
                      for a needle prick.

I cannot make any promises,
reassure our daughter about her parents' marriage.
Instead, I murmur regrets.
    Then ask, "What do you want for dinner?"

Letter to the Editor

I gotta stop writing you to the exclusion of all else
my house goes dirty the car unwashed the children
not fed and my husband wanders around the house
like a man with only the slimmest of clues and still
still still I find myself writing to you in distraction
wondering why in hell this attraction and when will
I end this one-sided correspondence anyway?

Writing Seduction Letters

Each of your carefully curated words
chosen to achieve your objective,
your irresistible lies pretty little demons
cluttering up the once pristine sheet.
If, in your passion, any sentence
threatens to expose you, or gets too close
to the real truth, hit the delete key, and begin again.

Reading Your Morning Horoscope

Over morning breakfast, you read your horoscope:
One who has broken a promise with impunity will suffer
the consequences.
You want to laugh the words off as cheap entertainment.
Astrology is a starry pseudo-science you remind yourself,
and gulp back bitter, cold coffee.

Yes, your days are now filled with broken truths. Lies pile up
like dirty dishes and unpaid bills, and this morning,
your betrayal is indelibly written in black ink on newsprint,
or like contraband letters waiting to be discovered by one
spouse, or the other.

Driving the Utah Desert, Children in the Backseat

Somewhere
beyond
pink
mountains
outside
this unfeeling
car
in which
you husband
and I
your wife
travel
as strangers
must wait
a heart-oasis
in this desert
where kindness
blooms
as wild
and free
as flowering
sego lilies

At a Rest Stop Between Butte and Missoula

If I pulled off to the side of the road
and gave birth to you at this rest stop
or crawled deep —
deeper than your flesh
was then lodged within my body—
like an animal crawling deep into your beloved woods
to crouch low beneath branches sheltering us
from florescent lights and masked doctors
and then licked you clean,
my tongue tasting your birth's blood
one thing would remain the same:
I would have loved you as fiercely
as I did in the hospital where you were born.
Only half as much as I do now.

A boy living in the suburbs,
you dream of roaming wild
and catching fish in flowing streams
with your bare hands or between your teeth.
From books you have learned the names and origins
of living things, insects and trees, lizards and frogs,
plants poisonous and safe: *bitterroot, huckleberry, beargrass*
Now you point out plants and fish to me
and I listen to you speak as the wind swirls between us
in this Montana rest stop so far
from the sterile hospital where you were born.
With each incantation: *cutthroat, whitefish, grayling*
I am stirred by something primal. Deep. Knowing.
I pay witness to your life. You to mine.

Soon, it will be time to go.

Coos Bay, Oregon

Was it the moment you and he stood together
on an observation deck overlooking the Oregon coastline,
the Pacific beating against the beach and nothing
but endless shades of gray reaching out in all directions,
until the not-quite-black specks of gulls
were less visible than The Incredible Shrinking Man
when his ego ceased to exist?

Did you stare in wonder
not at the bark of seals and squawk of gulls,
or the rush of waves   above   below   beyond
rocks older than any wisdom
you thought you had found
but at a man, who—

like a flower so uncommon
you cannot recall the name—

opens his petals only once or twice a year,
and then only when all conditions are perfect?

Opens his petals then quickly folds them inward again.

Why She Bought the Poet's Book

The boat house
stood sacred,
a chapel upon
the rocks.
No stained glass
could honor God
more than the clear
window overlooking
sea and sky
rock and shore
pelican and gull.
No sermon
could save
a sinner
(at least
this sinner)
like the poem
the poet read.
Some men
love their
wives
she thought
cheeks wet
with redemption.

But for the Lovers, Their Arms

In a letter, the woman quotes Heraclitus,
You can't step in the same river twice.

The man writes back, quoting Richard Brautigan,
the water in the river…knows what to do, flowing on.

The woman responds with a proverb,
Follow the river and you'll find the sea.

Because the hour is late, Dylan Thomas is mentioned.
No river found in this particular poem—

but the poet provides a moon that rages,
grieving lovers. Spindrift pages.

Poetry's black ink pales beneath a breaking heart,
and she forgets Langston's *soul has grown deep like a river.*

White river. White moon. The lovers' cold stone arms.
Her empty book. Unwritten letters. Bottled notes. Paper boats.

White fire her heart's secret grief—a barefoot ghost
wading into the river. Searching for the sea.

Poem title a line from "In My Craft or Sullen Art," by Dylan Thomas.

Blackberries

It was a night where poets spoke of blackberries
not vases & jewels, angry sons & fatherless daughters,
not philosophical questions about God's existence.
This night, blackberries burst open on vines,
scattered on the ground, gathered in aprons,
were bitten in two with tiny, sharp teeth.
In the brightly lit banquet hall, word-drunk poets
swallowed blackberry wine, burbled purple,
and sang odes to blackberries growing free
beneath warm and forgiving suns.
Outside, a thickening black night sky
waited, heavy with ferment.

Yes, tonight poems delivered joy.
Leaves, vines, and fleshy berries grew
in metaphor's pungent earth,
tangled around the poets' bare ankles,
and this commonplace word *blackberry*
served as a praise psalm, a prayer, an invocation,
a sacrament's dark sweet juices wetting thirsty lips
releasing the promise of wild geese & wing flash,
the scent of sea & summer grasses

Does poetry have any relation to the real world anyway?
The poets' room flowed its blackberry laughter.
Beneath the darkening sky's tough skin,
fruit grew bitter. Turned to poison.
Wine from the upset glass flowered into bruises.
Leaving violet stains that would never fade,
no matter how many poems were written.

What a Poem Cannot Do

A poem means less than bread to a starving man.

Words strung together to fashion a poem
does not create a safety net.

Poems are less effective than a mop in cleaning up blood.

His eye might be on the tiniest of sparrows,
but a bird still falls with crippled wing.

Tonight, I am done with poems.

White Clouds

Will poetry redeem anyone?
If the poet writes a poem about the horrors of war,
and someone hears it, will it be someone
who already accepts that war is horrible?
Will that someone have the power to stop such destruction?
Or will she take her pacifist views home
and turn the other cheek again, and again.
"Love me for who I am," everyone cries,
but do they love others in such a way?
Daily, the world grows more gray,
wraps itself around my ankles like a terrible weight.
The anxious and depressed slump around tables
in coffee houses, discuss their pain and drink more
caffeine—electro shock in a cup—pass the Prozac, please.
It would take more than a crane lift to haul
all the world's sorrows above the surface of the pit.
A Sufi said, "Why don't you write something uplifting?"
This suggestion could easily have been made by a Christian.
I still don't know how to answer.
I shrug my shoulders, scribble morose little poems
in cheap notebooks, worry about redemption,
and whether or not the world can be saved;
whether or not my children, my husband, my cousin,
my neighbor, myself can be saved.
In the morning, or in the midst of night,
I know that soon
tiny heartbeating birds will call to one another
from black branches and humming telephone lines.
White clouds with names I love to say,
   cumulus   nimbus   cirrus
will drift carefree
in a sky as blue as the eyes of my children

who will make me laugh in wonder
as I stroke a wayward lock of hair
or fix their peanut butter sandwiches.
Delighting again in the ways of children,
the ways of the world,
when young eyes are as clear as the sky is as blue
as the tranquil sea, poetry will once again rise
like a hymn of praise and salvation,
and not a wail of desolation.
   cumulus   nimbus   cirrus
Will this poem redeem itself?
Yes, just as certain as it will disappoint.

Avalanche

It is a heavy burden for any child to bear.
Each resentment a heavy stone added to the heap.

The yoke we all wear cuts deepest into her flesh.
Her tender back buckles beneath the load.

Daily car trips: to school or grocery store,
library or friend's home—fills us with new dread.

If her father drives, it is in stony silence.
Anger lodged in his petrified heart.

I drive with my hands clenching the wheel.
When I open my mouth to speak, rough pebbles

of complaint roll forth, gain momentum.
"I'm sorry," I tell my daughter.

Her small hand reaches out from beneath the rubble.
Strokes my arm. Speaks words of comfort. *To me.*

I bite my tongue in shame. Taste the bitter grit.
Choke back gravel.

Until the next drive—
when I open my mouth again.

Riding South on Interstate 70

I read a poem with the word October in its title.
Think of you. Imagine a man's strong, tender hands
hollowing out the shell of a pumpkin, and placing you
(as a tiny infant) in the gourd's thick cradle.

Those hands belong to your father,
bits and pieces of a man I can only imagine
(less than I can imagine you).

You never told me any story
about carving pumpkins with your father,
and I have never heard of a new moon infant boy
placed inside a pumpkin's womb.

I do not know what you looked like as a baby;
I do not know what you look like now.
I do not know what shape of hands
your father held you with,
but I do know that he held you.

You wrote in a letter you loved me.
I have not heard you say it,
but I know it true. A little.
The futility of love from such distances
scatters like autumn seeds upon bone-cold winds,
lands on ground that will not see harvest.

It is a sadness now bittersweet,
like an October moon waxing yellow
Above a field of orange pumpkins.

Perhaps I will take your letters
and plant them in the hard ground
behind my back door, and wait for fall.

Damaged Proof

torn fishnet stockings
gel-spiked hair
pouting lips

she leaves home in a fog
of cheap perfume:
I owe no explanation.

adrenaline heat surging
convulsive music pulsing
mosh pit frenzy

her heart rattles
its bony cage:
yes! yes! yes!

parking lot brawl cuts
bruised eye & swollen lip:
Look at me. I exist.

over breakfast
we mourn her
triumph.

Young Girl Lost on the Overpass

She wanders at 2 AM the overpass alone,
save for a roaring voice clamoring inside,
its discordant song louder than the swell
of traffic whizzing by down below.

A thin girl dressed in flannel pajamas,
empty pockets, and a man's black hoodie,
wandering not far from her childhood home.
A lost waif on the way to nowhere.

She does not see the round, white moon
glowing in the black sky or the glorious stars
in this galaxy from which she feels an outcast.

She does not notice her mother's car
slowing down, the beauty pulsing
inside her pain, or the celestial pinpricks
of light shining from above—

and years from now, her life,
her mother's life—all of their lives—
will not be the same lives they now carry.
Thanks to the voice inside her body
refusing to stay silent. Its razor cuts.

An Empty Table and Abandoned Chairs

How did it come to this?
Food left untouched. Grace unsaid.
Ignored, these gifts of the body are taken back.
Thirsting and hungry skin left to gather dust
in a forgotten closet. With no replenishment,
the heart's generosity ceases to flow, trickles down
to tiny measured amounts we do not drink.
The table and chairs, do they feel useless?
The rotting food, does it will itself to poison?
How much pain must be eaten?

The Uncoupling

This is our death, then.
You and I will soon cease to exist, coupled.
Beneath your rough exterior—
a good-looking man, I reassure you, and I mean it—
I catch brief glimpses of the boy I knew.
"Ollie ollie oxen free! Come out, come out, wherever you are!"
But it is not a carefree game of hide and seek.
We are no longer laughing children or joyous lovers
giving chase and surrendering delight.

You do not want to be found.

Our discarded playthings litter the unkempt yard.
Toys we have both outgrown, refuse to give away.
In anger, you stamp out the boy and crush the girl
with the deliberate heel of your boot.

Tears do not change a thing, give no comfort.

My throat fills with the dry,
unforgiving dust we find ourselves buried in.
Play no funeral march.
Music is filled with our past ghosts.
Resurrection might begin
when it is you and I, uncoupled.

Strawberries

I remember strawberry lips
beneath our cool, linen sheets.

How, sated and hungry, we pierced yielding flesh,
waiting for our desire to return, rest again.

How summer heat flowered on skin,
leaving tiny red thumbprints.

Now I consider how a fruit so sweet
could bruise and spoil quickly—

And how a faint strawberry scent is filled with regrets.

I Thought It Was Over Long Before It Was Done

Yes, I mistook the therapist's words as those of a prophet:
"You've done your grieving in the marriage."

I paid by the hour. It made sense to me.

Nothing, not even the old photograph of us
        captioned *First Road Trip Together*
could slow us down & stop the divorce proceedings.

Wearing silly grins, we thought we were grownups,
        our eyes hidden beneath can't shrink baseball caps.
                Where did those two children go?

Now we are strangers to one another,
        doing and getting things done.
                Not getting things done.
                      Trying, in vain,
                              to keep sorrow's truth

  at a distance.
        Stripped to its essence:
                      Loss.

                      Uncontested.

Bone, Exposed

Divorce papers were served to you
one Saturday morning while we were still in bed.

Year one, year two, year three, year four, and on…
       pink scraps of nothing
              pink scraps of everything
                      fluttering from your hands
     as you ripped the papers to shreds
before you spent an hour taping the document back together.

I've lost count of how many times during our separation
       we met at a hospital or grave site
             and recognizing one another's pain
                    we spoke words of comfort
     to one another, our hands afraid to touch.

I've lost count, too, of how many women
crossed the threshold of the house that was once our home.
Or how many times I never thanked the man, dead now,
      who dropped everything
            to come to our children's rescue.

The first year we married, your mother bought
a cross-stitch sampler stamped with a bride and groom
      in tiny x's—like kisses—above the words *Best Friends.*

She showed it to me after we argued
      in front of your parents at the table
           during one of our weekly dinners.
              "To be an anniversary gift."
                  Nothing else to say, she shrugged.

I've lost count of how many meals I ate at your family's house
   when we were still in high school.
      I didn't know happy marriages could exist,
         and longed to have a mother and father
         like yours—
            still together // still in love.

Year nineteen...
         the kit's needle and thread still untouched.

Just Like That

A woman cannot peel off nineteen years
of a marriage overnight

Strip herself as if removing sexy lingerie
her ex-husband once gave her.

Her body might respond to the new hands
caressing her neck with a shiver and cry

But she keeps its biggest secrets locked away:
Until Death Do You Part.

Her new lover says, "You don't wake up
one morning and tell yourself I am now

going to live with joy and it happens—
just like that."

Everyone Wants What They Want

"I refuse to live by anyone else's rules!"
An eighteen-year-old boy tells his single mother,

"Kick me out," he dares her, "I will live in the woods
and trap my own food."

In the same breath, the boy asks his mother
for a ride to the edge of the forest.

Beyond the small confines of their apartment's
well-stocked kitchen, the California sun

burns bright, threatens power outages: everyone wants
what they want when they want it.

A round, full moon wearing the face of a family therapist
peers in through their window.

"I must remain neutral," the face-in-the-moon cautions,
wearing an expression chalk white and knowing.

The boy's mother sees her parenting mistakes tallied
on the blackboard of her heart and her thoughts

circle through their city's neighborhoods and parking lots,
office buildings, fast food restaurants, and quickie marts—

What woods, she wonders.

At the Psychiatrist's Office

Through an open door,
while seated in a waiting room chair,
I glimpse a partially hidden view of Starry Night

magically, its thick eclipse exposes yellow sun & moon,
inky blues now streaking across canvas once the color
of clinical white walls.

It's only a print. One of many Van Gogh
reproductions stacked in shopping mall bins
across the country, thumb-tacked on dorm walls,
or framed in the homes of aspiring corporate types
with a fondness for the arts, doctors' offices, or here,
in the office of my teenage daughter's psychiatrist.

Printed posters everywhere, easy to overlook or
dismiss in the rush of ubiquitous overload,
not unlike breathing—forgotten—
until one forgets to breathe.

Look again.

Thick broad brushstrokes simple
until one notes the swirling complexity—
the giant fingerprints of God,
the bold genius of color gone mad.

This brief glimpse of a starry night escaping
through an open door that will soon close to swallow
my daughter, and her secrets, bruises my mother-heart
with new tenderness.

I think of my daughter's sad, lovely eyes
peering through her camera's view,
recognizing beauty in a hard world,
if only for a tiny starlit flicker,
before the dark of night descends,
and we wait for a new constellation to appear.

Thanksgiving Table

Tiger lilies flash orange petals
above the burnished wood table
where the glass vase rests.

Water rings cannot mar the table's beauty,
which once belonged to a friend in whose house
we sat around it drinking tea and telling secrets

Now smoke disappearing in a clear autumn sky.
In the white refrigerator, a slice of pumpkin pie
waiting to be devoured like a hungry poem.

Certain things make me think of you: the color orange,
silver planes flying overhead on my birthday,
October mornings, and circles of mouths

open wide, singing praise for friends unseen.
The woman on whose table I write this poem
now lives on a mountain with her new husband

a few hours and a lifetime away.
You and she were with me then.
You and she are with me now.

I eat up joy with each forkful of pie,
praising God, Richard Brautigan,
the moon, new beginnings, and all of you.

Remembering Birch Lake

Write it out.

Begin with the smallest thing:
    the hard, knotted piece
    of tree root
    exposed
    in damp,
    sparse grass

    your daughter's boot,
    which—if her foot moves
    just a breath—could easily
    crush the tiny frog beside it

    the mottled green
    and brown leaf
    that resembles
    your son's iguana,
    now tamed and renamed
    by another

    the water's startled center
    where strawberry rings ripple out
    until they disappear…

Write it out.

Begin again.

Epilogue

Like Festival Days

"...and festivals are as sunlit peaks,
testifying above dark valleys, to the eternal radiance."
—Clement A. Miles

I wash the strawberries and marvel at their beauty—
red and shaped not unlike the human heart.
Like festival days, only a few are blemished.
The rest are rich and full.

I leave the stems attached,
the green a striking contrast against the red.
I lovingly arrange them
on a bone-white plate
and place them on the table before our children.

Perhaps you drop by and we invite you in,
once again my friend.

All of us will eat with pleasure.

A Brief Note of Thanks

I am grateful to the many writing communities—then and now—who have included me in their commitment to craft and sharing our love of the written word.

I am also deeply grateful to the family, friends and work colleagues who helped me get through some very difficult times with such generosity and grace. I cannot name everyone, but a few individuals must be acknowledged: Andrew MacRae, Barbara Cole, Johnna Laird, Barbara Lyon, Christian Nelson, Larry Seeger, Janet Thomas, Joyce Dolores Weaver, and others whose names will surface in the middle of the night after this has gone to press.

Lines from an unfinished poem might express my gratitude best:

Each person I encounter who extends a kindness / at a needful time reminds me to drop to my knees and sing the praises / of those I have loved / those I love still / and who, fingering the bead of memory, / are with me still.

Thank you to my mother, who came through in ways I could never have imagined; and to my beloved Dan, now and always.

About the Author

Robin Michel (Pedersen) was born in Utah and moved to California at the age of seventeen. After her first marriage ended, Robin returned to school to earn her BA from Saint Mary's College and her MA from Mills College. She has over twenty-five years' experience working for nonprofits and in educational environments and is widely published in many different genres. Robin lives with her husband Dan Humphrey in San Francisco where they enjoy sharing their love of literature, art, music, and history with their brilliant grandchildren and other young people.